THOUGHTS ON MATHEMATICS

MATHEMATICS, MATHEMATICIANS, AND EDUCATION

FIRDOUS AHMAD MALA

Made with ♥ on the Notion Press Platform
www.notionpress.com

I dedicate this book to my Lord, the lord of the worlds.

Contents

Foreword

Mathematics has been extensively written on. From amusement to amazement, mathematics has a plethora of themes to offer us.

This is a collection of the author's six essays on themes related to mathematics.

Acknowledgements

I thank my wife, Asma Altaf for her encouragement and incessant support.

CHAPTER ONE

Finding a Place for Mathematics Education in Mathematics Curriculum

MATHEMATICS is one among several other human endeavours that have shaped the current state-of-the-art in science and technology. While, on the one hand, mathematics holds a key position in any curriculum, on the other hand, imparting mathematics instruction has remained a headache for almost all institutions, even at the university level.

It is not uncommon to find mathematicians not adept at the science of imparting instruction in mathematics. Charles Dodgson, aka Lewis Carroll, the author of Alice in Wonderland and Looking Through the Glass is reported to have found teaching extremely daunting. The prince of mathematics, Carl Friedrich Gauss is reported to have hated teaching for he believed that this way students robbed him of his precious time. He is later reported to have started enjoying it when the quality of students improved.

One of the finest mathematical brains of our time, Grigori Perelman who declined to accept the Fields Prize after cracking one of the hardest problems in mathematics, the Poincaré Conjecture has been reported to have quit his position at the Steklov Institute in 2005 because he finds mathematics a painful topic to discuss.

This situation is grim and disheartening. Those who have had the chance to watch the movie, The Beautiful Mind might remember how awful a teacher John Nash was depicted to have been at Princeton. The fact remains that all good scholars are not good teachers. In fact, some excellent scholars and researchers, such as those mentioned above have proved to be pathetic at instruction and dissemination of information.

Is there a cure? A remedy? Perhaps, yes.

Calculus, Analysis, Combinatorics and Geometry are not all there is to mathematics. In the words of Ian Stewart, one of the finest popularizers of mathematics of the time, "During the past fifty years, more mathematics has been created than in all previous ages put together". Given the quantum of research articles produced every year and the dismal situation of instruction in Higher Educational Institutions (HEIs), the question of didactics becomes a highly serious issue and concern in mathematics. We are in dire need of exceptional teachers. For that, we need to introduce or embrace Mathematics Education and find a respectable place for it in our already-vague-and-confusing curriculum of mathematics. Mathematics Education is the practice of teaching and learning mathematics, alongside the associated research. It is the knowledge of how, what, when, where and why of teaching mathematics.

In 2015, a project called the INDRUM (International Network for Didactic Research in University Mathematics) was established the primary aim of which is to contribute to the development of research in mathematical didactics at all levels of university education. In the three INDRUM conferences held thus far in 2016, 2018 and 2020, a decent exchange of ideas has taken place and a lot of good quality research has been shared in this regard. In a recent 2021 Springer publication titled "Research and Development in University Mathematics Education," several key points of these INDRUM conferences have been put in understandable words that may help us distinguish mathematicians from mathematics educationists.

One particular research discussed in this book is regarding the current status of didactics in mathematics in some countries including Australia, and the USA. In Australia, there is a clear divide between mathematicians and mathematics educators. This divide, however, does not exist in the USA. As a matter of fact, in the United States, mathematics education positions and one-third of the doctoral programmes are offered in Mathematics Education. The Aussies, however, are now beginning to understand the way forward. They are rectifying the mistakes and acknowledging that Mathematics Education is becoming indispensable and urgent.

The condition of our HEIs is disappointing. Each academic year, hundreds if not thousands of postgrads are handed degrees with which they hardly know what to do. They are hardly acquainted enough with the subject to become good instructors given that the forerunners are themselves not deep-rooted in the ins and outs of instruction.

Over a course of more than a decade of mathematics teaching at elementary, school and higher levels, it has dawned upon me that merely perfecting mastery over the content we teach is not going to make our teaching desirably better. We need to embrace Mathematics education and learn the tricks of the trade before we torrent theorems and exercises at our students.

Unfortunately, teaching positions are decided based on how well someone has done in academics and research and not on an assessment of how much the candidate is in love with the subject. In the words of M. E. Sangster, “No one should teach who is not in love with teaching”.

The art of instruction is holier and harder to master than reaching a scholarly position bereft of skills and compassion. It takes a big heart to shape little minds.

CHAPTER TWO

The Unconventional Case of Crowdsourcing Mathematics

Mathematics is both an individual activity and a collaborative one. Who could forget the contributions of Pythagoreans to mathematics? They seem to have been the staunchest believers in the power of numbers. From the music of planets to theology and theorems to doctrines, they are supposed to have utilized numbers in numerous walks of human life. They attempted to interpret almost everything via numbers, including music and friendship. Due to their collaborative efforts, they could see what others could not get a glimpse of. In the words of Richard Tarnas, "The forms of mathematics, the harmonies of music, the motions of the planets, and the gods of the mysteries were all essentially related for Pythagoreans, and the meaning of that relation was revealed in an education that culminated in the human soul's assimilation to the world soul, and thence to the divine creative mind of the universe."

This is not an isolated incident in the history of mathematics. In our times, with the advent of new technologies and new platforms, several new concepts have come to the fore. And one such concept is that of the PolyMath Project or crowdsourcing mathematics knowledge.

The idea of crowdsourcing mathematics may come to many as a case of daydreaming. However, as good luck would have it, crowdsourcing mathematics is not just possible but an already-achieved feat. It goes back to January 2009 when Timothy Gowers, a British mathematician, posted a problem on his blog with a strange but beautiful idea of crowdsourcing its solution online. He solicited the help of everyone to contribute, either entirely or partially, to a possible solution to the problem. This was in itself a highly innovative and massive invitation. This project came to be known as the Polymath Project.

Amazingly, the efforts were successful, and the problem was solved via an immense online collaboration of amateur and professional mathematicians. The solution to the mathematical problem originally posted by Gowers was arrived at not very long after it was originally posted. That is the power of working in unison. Along with the actual problem, Gowers is reported to have posted a question in the blog: Is massively collaborative mathematics possible? The answer, now, of course, is yes.

This ushered in an era of new possibilities, and several other initiatives followed soon after. One such initiative is the CrowdMath project targeted at benefitting high school and college students. As per the Art of Problem Solving website, popularly known as AoPS Online, last accessed on 13th May 2022,

"CrowdMath is an open project that allows all high school and college students to collaborate on a large research project with top-tier research mentors and an exceptional peer group. MIT PRIMES and Art of Problem Solving are working together to create a place for students to experience research mathematics and discover ideas that did not exist before." As is obvious, it envisions creating a congenial platform for high school and college students to do better in their mathematical endeavors and in helping them marvel and get exposed to the world of mathematical research.

Besides online collaborations, there is another world from which one can learn mathematics. Gone are the days when one was required to travel miles to see a mathematics expert. With the possibility of online and distance learning, one can relish the taste of learning without caring about the distance and the expenses. There exist numerous online platforms where one can learn from and engage with mathematicians from all over the world. Such platforms facilitate the exchange of high-quality mathematical communication and expose the naïve to the best in the business. MathStackExchange and MathOverFlow are two such online places.

Besides these, numerous YouTube channels, such as Krista King, Brian McLogan, MySecretMathTutor, ProfRobBob, PatrickPMT, and 3Blue1Brown, contribute to the spread of much-needed mathematical awareness. These are some of the most awesome mathematics channels where one can learn high-quality mathematics from the ease of one's home.

Remember that for any society to be recognized in these technological times, the role of mathematics is tough to overestimate. The progress of a community could be measured by the amount of mathematics known and put to use by its individuals and its masses. And doing mathematics is not as expensive as doing other types of research. In the words of George Polya, "Mathematics is the cheapest science. Unlike physics or chemistry, it does not require any expensive equipment. All one needs for mathematics is a pencil and paper."

CHAPTER THREE

On Devlin's Death of Mathematics

This write-up draws on the opinions of Doctor Keith Devlin expressed in the essay "The Death of Mathematics". Devlin is a professor of mathematics at Stanford University and has authored several books including The Language of Mathematics, The Man of Numbers, and The Unfinished Game, among many others. He is also known for his online visibility. His course titled Introduction to Mathematical Thinking, offered by Coursera is one of the most celebrated Massive Open Online Courses (MOOCs) on Mathematics. In all, he is someone who knows quite well what it means to teach mathematics both offline and online. Devlin, in his essay, points to a very enervating question. He drives our attention to a very sensitive issue. This is the question of the death of mathematics, and the subsequent impact on human life and its flourishing.

In his essay, Devlin makes readers realize that advances in science, engineering, technology, and management are heavily dependent upon advances in mathematics. Mathematics kind of reshapes them over and over again. It is indispensable for human progress and human flourishing. No mathematics would have serious and ugly implications.

To understand what the death of mathematics means, consider the following. The question of whether technology should be embraced and welcomed without scrutinizing it and without weighing its pros and cons is a common concern. Given the number of gadgets at our disposal, there is a double-edged sword staring us right in the face. Not embracing the technology of the times is like denying oneself the pleasures and benefits of human advancements on the one hand, and, on the other hand, there is an invariable danger of falling prey to it and playing in the hands of technology.

In the essay, Devlin points to the transition or shift in which people turned to using calculators and computers for carrying out mathematical calculations. While on one hand, the use of such mechanical aids did do away with some of the basic abilities to do mathematics sums in mind or using pen and paper, yet, on the other hand, arithmetic skills gave way to algebraic thinking. So, it was not a complete disaster.

Devlin is, however, deeply concerned with the danger that lies in the excessive use of such devices. The advent of sophisticated machinery at hand for carrying out both complicated and basic calculations in mathematics has made it next to impossible that us to witness again the likes of mathematical gems such as Fermat, Gauss, Riemann, and Ramanujan. The habit of carrying out tedious and long calculations by hand dawned upon them a deep understanding of the behavior of numbers and it resulted in several beautiful and insightful conjectures in mathematics.

But the beauty of having machines do calculations, which otherwise would have not been easy or even in some cases humanly possible even for the mathematical giants is also not a petty thing. Machines can find out quickly what we may not be able to do even in years together.

This is a dilemma where one has to either do away with the traditional methods of learning and doing mathematics with pen and paper, or else, do away with the technology of the times. The latter seems not possible.

For Devlin, it is devastating and destroying if the tradition of doing mathematics by hand goes for good. Devlin is somewhat unsure of what is going to happen to mathematics given such circumstances. And he seems, almost surely, to believe that this way, mathematics is going to die an unfortunate death. To him, it is not going to be very long, just a couple of decades. And if that happens, all genuine progress is going to be halted. The death of mathematics is going to leave science, technology, engineering, and all other forms of human domains affected beyond repair.

We may choose to embrace the technology of our times and do away with pen and paper. But then, we need to gauge the possible danger that lies in such adoption. Our educational institutions are becoming more and more paperless. Tabs, screens, online or digital learning management systems, and streaming of content are becoming increasingly popular and commonplace. It may be a good thing. It may be a bad thing. We need to weigh the pros and cons. We need to strike a balance.

Calculators have their roles to play and humans have bigger roles to play. Humans cannot afford to give away the power of being creative and innovative by falling prey to their own inventions. In the words of John A. Wan de Walle, “Calculators can only calculate - they cannot do mathematics.” Although the advent of artificial intelligence has made it possible that machines may come up with mathematical conjectures and many other surprising things, it seems like a man will have to bear the burden of being creative. Humans cannot afford to bring the world to a standstill. Humans must do mathematics.

CHAPTER FOUR

A Mathematician's Social Plight

Have you ever thought about what it means to think or behave logically in a world that is overpopulated by illogical and unreasonable people? Do you believe that being logically upright and argumentatively valid comes cheap? Have you ever considered the difficulties and dangers that a mathematician is forced to face diurnally?

A person's endeavours are likely to impact him. A person's habits and undertakings continually shape or reshape his personality. Studying a subject as rigorous as mathematics is akin to bringing certain changes in one's behaviour and attitude. The kind of everyday thinking and reasoning that is needed in mathematics impacts a reader's perspective and his very disposition. Mathematics kind of reshapes the attitude, the behaviour, the conduct and the deportment of the one who studies it. It embellishes, furbishes, garnishes and harnesses the very self of the one who undertakes its study.

Defining precisely what constitutes the subject matter of mathematics may be hard. The fact remains that it is no less hard to define the life of a mathematician. The life of a mathematician is a mystery in its own right. Mathematicians are known for being precise or to the point. Rigour is a hallmark of mathematics and proof is not considered a burden but rather a confirmation, a thing of beauty. A mathematician is not burdened by the requirement of proof; rather, he kind of enjoys and relishes the very taste of it. A mathematician is a citizen of the world of proof and rigour. He values truth beyond boundaries. In the words of David Hilbert, "Mathematics knows no races or geographical boundaries; for mathematics, the cultural world is one country."

Mathematics, being an interplay of logic and language, impacts those who engage with it. In the words of Johann Wolfgang von Goethe, "Mathematicians are like Frenchmen: whatever you say to them they translate into their language and forthwith it is something entirely different." This leads to a very crucial point, that of precision and symbolism. Note that, owing to its very nature and style, mathematics is often written using symbols. This makes it similar to a language, though a symbolic one. People not well-versed with the language struggle with it. This results in further separation between a mathematician and the society he dwells in.

The lives of hundreds of mathematicians who have come to pass in this world have had a profound and prominent impact on the thought process of their contemporaries and their antecedents. The likes of Pythagoras, Euclid, Euler, Gauss, Cauchy, Riemann, Hardy, Russell and Godel have left lasting impressions on their readers. Remember that writing mathematics is not like writing in other disciplines. A writer may have to mind himself while writing in other disciplines; but in mathematics, a writer has added responsibilities of being logical, correct and meticulous besides being required to be more mindful of what he is writing. This is because you can neither appeal to authority, nor can you appeal to emotions or multitude or beg the question. This means that mathematicians while writing mathematics exercise a lot of caution, precision and brevity, besides making sure the ubiquity of authenticity, proof and validity.

History is witness to the unwelcome treatment meted out to those who resorted to being mathematical in their approach. It should not take one very long to gauge the danger that lies in being logical and mathematical in a world populated by masses that have little or nothing to do with logic and mathematical rigour. The fact remains that most people either do not concern themselves with mathematics and logic or live with some wrong or incorrect understanding of them. This culminates in a painful and struggling situation. A mathematician has to survive every day between logic and waywardness. He has to balance himself between the truth and the falsehood. A mathematician lives a comprising life with his fellow men who have no inclination towards being concerned, meticulous and circumspect of their utterances, words or actions. A mathematician cannot afford to be himself in a society that would not understand him or would not appreciate being informed, in the face, that they resort to incorrect use of language and beside-the-mark understanding of words. He may not, mostly, be allowed to pinpoint the fallacies in others' arguments. He has to, on the one hand, learn and master the rigour needed for enriching mathematical knowledge; and on the other hand, he has to see the same rigour being not taken care of by his fellow beings. He has to face all of this. He has to live with the dilemma. Man does not live by mathematics and logic alone.

Another issue that a mathematician has to confront on a day-to-day basis is that of not being able to make others understand their pitfalls and aberrations. Sometimes, even the blunders of people go unnoticed if neither the speaker nor the listener is mindful of the knowledge of logic and rigour. However, that should not be taken to mean that a mathematician's life is dull or less adventurous. The thrill of a mathematical discovery or the joy of solving a mathematical problem is ineffable. In the words of Bertrand Russell, "The pure mathematician, like the musician, is a free creator of his world of ordered beauty."

Do not ever live under the false impression that you are logical if you are not. Test your logic. Learn the rudiments of logic and appreciate the rigour of mathematics. The invitation and the doors are always open. The largest room in the world is the room for improvement. One way to do that is to grab a source such as a book or a teacher, an expository article or a discussion with a learned person. In a world overpopulated by people that lack reason and logic, make efforts to upgrade yourself to become not just a rational being but a mathematically logical being, and thereby help give rise to more meaning and more understanding for an intellectually healthier, satisfying and meaningful coexistence.

CHAPTER FIVE

Understanding what Russell said about Mathematics

Known for his mathematics, logic, and philosophy and honored for his contributions to the field of literature, Bertrand Russell is famous as one of those who has had a prominent influence on several subjects of study and has discussed the intricacies that otherwise would have been hard to even catch sight of or get wind of. Although he is known for being a philosopher, yet, he was unlike a lot of them. He considered and maintained that logic is not a part of philosophy.

"Logic, it must be admitted, is technical in the same way as mathematics is, but logic, I maintain, is not part of philosophy," Russell famously wrote. "Philosophy proper deals with matters of interest to the general educated public, and loses much of its value if only a few professionals can understand what is said."

British Nobel Laureate and polymath, Bertrand Russell wrote, "Mathematics, rightly viewed, possesses not only truth, but supreme beauty – a beauty cold and austere, like that of sculpture, without appeal to any part of our weaker nature, without the gorgeous trappings of painting or music, yet sublimely pure, and capable of a stern perfection such as only the greatest art can show."

In what follows, an attempt is made at a brief analysis of this infamous quote of his.

At the very outset, we are made to acknowledge the importance of being earnest. We are driven to believe in the premise of having the right approach. To Russell, mathematics must be "rightly viewed". Viewing mathematics rightly means getting the essence of it. It means that one must appreciate and understand mathematics rather than get lost in its symbolism and calculations. One must appreciate the ideas woven in the language of mathematics rather than merely looking for computations and algorithms.

In the words of the Field Medalist, William Thurston, "Mathematics is not about numbers, equations, computations, or algorithms: it is about understanding."

The next thing Russell mentions is the fact that mathematics possesses both truth and beauty. To Russell, mathematics possesses truth and that is not an astonishing claim. However, mathematics possesses beauty and not everyone can see or appreciate that beauty.

It is pertinent to mention that truth, beauty and goodness have been the sought of the philosophers. In the words of Albert Einstein written long back in 1930 in his essay, What I believe: "The ideals which have always shone before me and filled me with the joy of living are goodness, beauty, and truth."

It is not strange that the virtues of truth and beauty have been discussed by Russell as mathematics cannot and must not be considered completely irrelevant to philosophy. Interestingly, something similar was opined by Einstein: "The pursuit of truth and beauty is a sphere of activity in which we are permitted to remain, children, all our lives."

Moving on, we find that Russell draws a liking between the beauty mathematics possesses and the beauty of a sculpture. He calls this beauty "cold" and "austere". However, he kind of chooses and prefers a sculpture to a painting or a piece of music. Russell makes a mention of paintings and music. But, he seems to be not impressed by them. He seems to be unmoved and not tempted by their attraction and calls that attraction "trappings".

Sculptures have been known for their durability, longevity and their beauty. A sculpture is more like the real in comparison to a painting that provides just a two-dimensional view. Though one might argue that paintings are no less beautiful than sculptures, the fact, however, remains that, to Russell, paintings and music are somewhat less beautiful and somewhat derogatory compared to sculptures.

Towards the end, we observe one important thing. We are made to note Russell's claim that art is capable of a certain perfection. He believes that mathematics is capable of perfection too. Russell is not very different from John Locke's assertion about mathematics. To Locke, "Mathematics is a way to settle in the mind a habit of reasoning."

In the words of Russell, "Mathematics takes us into the region of absolute necessity, to which not only the actual word, but every possible word, must conform."

To sum it up, we are able to read between the lines and see how Russell was capable of weaving together his acumen, his knowledge of literature and different arts and coming up with beautifully interwoven subtle observations that are probably not cups of coffee for everyone.

CHAPTER SIX

Fields Medalists 2022

For reasons not worth disclosure and not fit for the current discussion, there is no Nobel Prize for mathematicians. But there are prizes no less prestigious than the Nobel Prize. There is the Abel Prize and there is the Fields Prize.

The Fields Medal is awarded as recognition to young mathematicians who are not over forty but have done work in mathematics that deserves applause and appreciation.

This year, the Fields Medal was given to four mathematicians in recognition of their work and findings. Among them is a female mathematician from Ukraine, who became only the second woman ever to have received the Medal.

June Huh, a Korean American mathematician, is a professor at Princeton University. He has also taught at Stanford University and the Institute for Advanced Study. His work concerning algebraic geometry and combinatorics has been hard to be missed. In his words, "In practice what motivates us to pursue our goals is the pursuit of beauty." To him, it is not the applications but the internal beauty that makes mathematicians like him strive and appreciate pure mathematics. He received the Medal for the connections he found that exist between geometry and combinatorics. His story has nicely been woven into words by Kevin Hartnett in Quanta Magazine's "A Path Less Taken to the Peak of the Math World".

Hugo Duminil-Copin, another 2022 Fields Medalist, is a French mathematician who specializes in probability theory. Phys.org has come up with a nicely written article on him wherein it is mentioned how he goes about his work and his workplace. At merely 31, he was appointed professor at France's Institute of Advanced Scientific Studies in 2016. He has had the privilege to study under Stanislav Smirnov, another Fields Medalist. He speaks and lectures in French, and is so down to earth that once he came to know about the recognition of his feat, he remarked that he "does not really fit in the clichés of a genius". Hugo credits part of his success to the environment that makes it possible for him to go at his own pace without much obligations and workload. The Paris Institute is known to allow its researchers to free themselves of all obligations, thereby paving way for success such as in his case. Jordana Cepelewicz has written a wonderful write-up on his work and his way in Quanta Magazine's "For His Sporting Approach to Math, a Fields Medal".

James Maynard, a British number theorist, and this year's Fields Medal recipient, has done his work in prime numbers and the gaps between them. A prime is a counting number that has exactly two divisors. The fascination with prime numbers has gripped a thousand mathematical souls. Be it Euclid or Fermat, Hardy or Ramanujan, primes have held the attention of mathematicians over generations. From their infinitude as reported by Euclid to the arbitrary large gaps between them, we have witnessed a plethora of intriguing yet revealing idiosyncrasies of primes. And Maynard has added more to the surprises. Maynard is reported to have established with proof that there are infinitely many primes that do not involve the digit 7. Quantum Magazine in its article titled "A Solver of the Hardest Easy Problems about Prime Numbers" has come up with a detailed account of his achievement as a pretty young mathematician who is merely 35 right now.
Maryna Viazovska, a Ukrainian mathematician, is the only female mathematician after the Iranian maestro, Maryam Mirzakhani, to be included in the list of Fields Medal recipients. She is a full professor at the Institute of Mathematics of the Ecole Polytechnique in Switzerland. Her work in sphere-packing in the eighth dimension, which made her a Fields Medal recipient, has given the inhabitants of Kyiv in Ukraine a reason to smile despite the ongoing war. She is also reported to have collaborated with others and solved the sphere-packing problem in dimension 24. Quantum Magazine has beautifully summed up her struggle and her mathematics in "In Times of Scarcity, War and Peace, a Ukrainian Finds the Magic in Math". There is much to learn from how people like these go about their work with sincerity and devotion. It seems as if the beauty of mathematics that was likened to the beauty of a sculpture by Bertrand Russell is what a mathematician is supposed to strive for. Mathematics is not just the study of numbers and figures; it is a pursuit of beauty and, obviously, truth.

Printed by Libri Plureos GmbH in Hamburg,
Germany